Nancy Tel[fer]

Singing
In Tune

strategies & solutions for conductors,
conductors-in-training, & voice teachers

Special thanks to:
Deral Johnson and Constance Newland
for sharing their insights of good intonation,
and to Angela Wakeford and Glenn Taylor
for their suggestions for improvements in this book.

Nancy Telfer has been one of the major influences in choral singing in the last decade. She has improved reading and vocal skills in thousands of choirs through her publications *Successful Sight-Singing Books 1 & 2*, and *Successful Warmups Books 1 & 2*. Her skill of analyzing problems and creating solutions was developed during her many years as a choral and band conductor.

Ms. Telfer continues her work with choirs and conductors through presenting workshops and adjudicating. She is continually in demand as a commissioned composer. Her degree in Music Education and Theory and Composition is from the University of Western Ontario.

She resides with her family in the Toronto area.

ISBN 0-8497-4187-4

Contents

Introduction

Good intonation is an invaluable asset to a choir; it is essential in the creation of an inspiring performance. When a choir sings out of tune, the audience is intensely aware of the problem. Even though the phrasing may be beautifully shaped, the tone quality heavenly, and the diction excellent, intonation problems can eat away at the pleasure the audience would normally experience while hearing such accomplishments.

Although some singers seem to have natural tuning skills, good intonation is actually an acquired skill: singers **learn** how to tune their voices. Even singers with good general intonation have occasional problems. In order to assist the singers in the development of their intonation skills, conductors can work with the singers in three areas:

1. *Awareness:* Singers should learn to identify intonation problems as they occur.
2. *Analysis:* After developing a knowledge of the causes of poor intonation, a singer can learn how to determine the reason for a specific intonation problem in a piece of music.
3. *Correction:* Singers can learn strategies that will help them to correct a problem or even prevent such a situation arising in the future.

The singers must understand that intonation is important but it is ultimately the responsibility of the conductor to be consistent in keeping the standard high. A conductor who constantly listens to the intonation develops a taste for well-tuned music. Whenever the choir sings out of tune, it reinforces poor tuning in the ears of the singers. When the conductor insists on good intonation, the singers become accustomed to producing and hearing music in tune; they soon learn to accept nothing but the best.

With some repertoire and in some acoustical situations, tuning can be hard work. A choir can tire very quickly when working on intonation problems. A great deal of concentration and energy is required to practice good intonation. The choir should work intensely on good intonation skills for a few moments and then go on to some other aspect of the music. The choir can return to intensive work on intonation later in the rehearsal. A number of short, productive sessions on tuning is much more valuable than one long session.

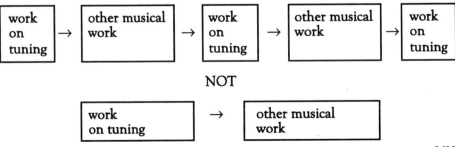

The time spent developing good intonation is a wise investment. With good tuning, the singers:

- Enjoy the rehearsals much more;
- Have better general stamina (out-of-tune singing can tire the ears more quickly than any other problem!);
- Can learn music at an interesting level of difficulty;
- Will have the freedom to concentrate more on other aspects of the music.

And the final results of the performance are so much more satisfying.

I. Causes of Poor Intonation

When an intonation problem has been identified, it is important to understand the cause(s) of the problem. There are a number of reasons why singers have difficulty with intonation.

Sometimes more than one factor may be causing poor intonation. When the strongest factor is corrected, the other factors may automatically adjust. Each chapter of this book outlines strategies and activities to correct intonation problems in different situations.

General Topic for Solutions	Cause of Poor Intonation	Solutions Appear on Pages
Accompaniment	Unaware of accompaniment	22, 59-60, 66-68
	Piano not ideally located	66
	Accompaniment is overly complicated	25-26
	Organ registrations	68
Acoustics	Poor acoustics	26, 72
Awareness	Unaware of a problem	12
	Cannot distinguish flat tuning from sharp	13-14
Conductors	Tense choral environment	14, 43
	Inappropriate gestures	43, 60
	Poor conductor's posture	43, 71
Dynamics	Singers are too loud to hear other parts . .	14, 21, 23-24, 26
	Faulty concept of *forte* or *piano*	50-52
	Faulty vocal production	47-49, 52
	Slow tempo	47
	Changing dynamics	53-54
	Loud, rhythmic music	64
Environment (Physical)	Too hot, too cold or humid	34, 71
	Tight clothing or shoes	34
	Overcrowding	34
Flat Singing	Slouching body	11, 62
	Vocal production problems	17, 27, 29-36, 61-62
	Vowel color	45
	Position of the mouth	45
	Soft dynamics	47-51, 72
	Diminuendo	53-54
	Lack of energy	55
	Descending music	63
	Slow tempo	65, 72
	Seating plan	70
	Conductor's posture	71

General Topic for Solutions	Cause of Poor Intonation	Solutions Appear on Pages
Harmony	Not harmonizing	20
	Not hearing the harmonic framework	21-22, 71
	Unfocused tone for close harmony	24
	Key changes	23-24
High Pitches	Inappropriate vowels	15
	Tense throat	57-58
	Exposed choral parts	59-60
	Voices not warmed up	57
	Lack of stamina	58-59
Listening Skills	Inattention to important melodic pitches	18-19
	Inattention to the harmony	20-24
	Ignorance of function of scale pitches	19
	Inability of a singer to hear own voice	16-17
	Overloaded ears	25-26
	Unaware of physical sensation of chord	16-17
	Unaware of accompaniment	22, 59-60, 68
Low Pitches	Voices not warmed up	61
	Voice placement too far back	61-62
	Dark timbre	62
Lyrics	Poorly chosen lyrics	15
	Improper pronunciation of vowels	44-45
	Vowels/diphthongs not uniform	44
	Improper use of consonants	45-46
	Fast, rhythmic music	64
Pitch Contour	Inability to tune repeated pitches	13-14
	Awkward intervals	15
	Unnatural pitch contour	15
	Floating melodies	15
	Ignorance of the structural pitches	18-19
	Ignorance of the function of pitches	19
	Close melodic intervals	19
	Ascending and descending music	63
Posture	Unbalanced or slouching body	10-11, 35
	Body tension	10, 34, 37-43
	Poor head position	35, 62, 69
Preparation	Scores not marked	18, 24, 56, 67-68
Psychological Factors	Shyness	35-36
	Nervousness	72
	Inadequate concert experience	72
	Tense environment	14, 34, 42-43

General Topic for Solutions	Cause of Poor Intonation	Solutions Appear on Pages
Repertoire	Poorly chosen lyrics/Badly crafted music ..	15
	Ascending/Descending music	63
	Inappropriate key signature	15
	Too much high-pitched music	57-58
Rhythm	Unnatural rhythms	15
	Rapidly changing pitches	64
Seating Plan	Straight rows	69
	Too many or too few rows	69-70
	No risers	70
	Unsuitable voices side-by-side	70-71
	Too crowded	34
	Singers cannot hear each other	26, 71
Sharp Singing	Tension	37-43, 71-72
	Vowel color	45
	Poor vocal production	27-28
	Crescendo	53-54
	Ascending music	63
	Fast tempo	65, 72
Sustained Notes	Unbalanced body	10-11
	Inappropriate vowels	15
	Poor vocal energy	31, 55
	High pitch	59-60
Tempo	Soft music	47
	Slow music	65
	Fast tempo with abundant words	64
	Wrong tempo	72
Vocal Production	Inadequate air pressure or air flow	11, 29-30, 47
	Unfocused tone	19, 24, 26, 28, 49, 61
	Tone too dark or too bright	45, 61-62
	Vocal placement - too low in the mouth	11, 33-34, 44
	- too far back in the head	26, 31, 33, 48, 52, 61
	Lack of resonance; improper use of overtones	11, 27, 31-32, 34, 36-38
	Poor vocal energy	31, 45-46, 48-49, 53, 55, 67
	Soft palate not raised	31-32, 35
	Mouth partially closed	35, 48
	Mouth open sideways	45
	Tension in throat, tongue, shoulders or arms	10-11, 34, 37-43, 52, 57-58, 60, 69, 71-72
	Excessive vibrato	70
Warmups	Voices not warmed up	57, 61

II. Posture and Intonation

Singers should learn the fundamentals of good posture before they begin work on intonation. Good posture sets the scene for good intonation. When the body is in the best position for singing, it is also in the best position for listening.

A Balanced Body

When the singer's balance is unstable, the tuning is unstable. When the body is balanced, it is easier for the singer to:

- Listen to the sound coming from the rest of the choir;
- Concentrate on evaluating his or her own tuning;
- Begin a note in tune;
- Keep sustained notes steady in pitch;
- Match the tuning of two identical pitches.

Teach your singers to be balanced in every aspect of posture:

Legs slightly apart: If the legs are too close together, the body tends to waver as the singer becomes involved in the music. When the body is unsteady, the tuning tends to be unsteady.

Weight balanced sideways between the two legs: When the weight is almost all on one leg, that leg becomes rigid and, before long, the upper body (including the throat) becomes tense. Tension can create a variety of problems with intonation.

Weight balanced from front to back: If a singer is constantly leaning slightly forward onto the toes or backward onto the heels, the body is not in an ideal position. When the body is balanced from the front to the back, the singer has enough flexibility to make adjustments in the tuning. Singers should be encouraged to wear shoes with low heels that do not push the weight forward on the toes.

It is not a good idea to place one foot forward because, although the body may be balanced from front to back, the singer has less control in the balance from side to side.

Head straight: If the head is leaning to one side, it is awkward to find the correct vocal placement for each pitch; this can affect the tuning dramatically.

■ **Strategy:** *Have the singers find the center of their balance by starting with an unbalanced position and then feeling the contrast as they move to a balanced position. Use a rhythmic approach to make posture more enjoyable.*

■ **Activity:**
Place the feet as far apart as the width of the shoulders. Move to a slow beat starting with the legs as suggested on the next page.

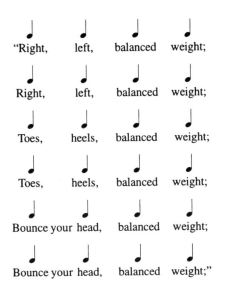

"Right,	left,	balanced	weight;
Right,	left,	balanced	weight;

Gently bounce the weight first on the right leg, then the left leg, then twice on both legs together. Repeat.

Toes,	heels,	balanced	weight;
Toes,	heels,	balanced	weight;

Lean the weight slightly forward onto the toes, then backwards onto the heels, then bounce twice with the body balanced. Repeat.

Bounce your head,	balanced	weight;
Bounce your head,	balanced	weight;"

Bounce the weight of the head slightly to the right, then the left, then twice with the head centered. Repeat.

A Slouching Body

When the torso caves inward at the front, the lungs are not able to inflate properly. At the same time, the abdominal muscles are not able to control the air flow to sustain the note and keep the intonation steady.

When the entire body is sagging, the singers:

- Find it difficult to create air pressure;
- Tend to sing from the bottom of the mouth (that "down in the mouth" feeling!);
- Do a poor job of activating the resonance in most of the head.

Each of these problems can lead to flat singing.

■ **Strategy:** *Have the singers "inflate" their bodies by gradually filling up with energy.*
■ **Activity for singers:**
  a) Take one slow breath while imagining that one part of the body is filling up with energy.
  b) Release the air as a focused stream directed into the distance.
  c) Repeat the activity with other parts of the body.
     Fill the legs with energy, then release the air.
     Fill the arms with energy, then release the air.
     Fill the torso... the head . . . the full body . . . .

■ **Strategy:** *Have each singer manipulate the shoulders to relax the chest into a singing position.*
■ **Activity for singers:**
  Slowly roll both shoulders in circles: forward, up, and back. Repeat several times.

III. Awareness of Poor Intonation

Locating the Problem

First of all, the singers must learn to notice exactly when the music is out of tune. When singers have structured practice in identifying the location of tuning problems, they become more aware of out-of-tune singing in general. When the singers are aware of the exact location of a problem, they can be prepared to automatically adjust the pitch if the problem should reoccur.

■ **Strategy:** *A conductor can bring an intonation problem to the attention of the singers by calmly identifying the location of a specific problem in the music.*

■ **Activity:**

Briefly comment on the measure(s) with poor tuning: e.g. "Did you hear the pitch start to sink at measure 26?"

Then give the singers an opportunity to correct the problem. Be sure to acknowledge any success even if the tuning is still not perfect.

Whenever possible, the error should be identified as either sharp or flat so that the singers will learn the difference.

When the singers' attention is directed toward an intonation problem, their awareness of tuning suddenly becomes more acute. Because anything that is highlighted in a rehearsal gains greater importance, the singers begin to take responsibility for listening for intonation problems.

■ **Strategy:** *Instead of pinpointing the measures with poor intonation, you can ask the singers to determine when the music goes out of tune on a specific page.*

This strategy takes more time in the short term but it saves time in future rehearsals because singers learn how to identify the location of a problem.

■ **Activity:**

After the choir has sung a passage of music:

a) Ask the singers where the music is going out of tune.

b) Repeat the passage to determine the answer to the question. Several things may happen:
   • Because the singers are listening more carefully, the tuning may automatically improve;
   • Some singers may be able to pinpoint the problem bar;
   • Some singers may be able to guess the reason for the intonation problem. e.g. They may hear that their own choral part is going flat in a specific measure or they may realize that as another part becomes flat the remainder of the choir adjusts the pitch downwards.

Determining Whether the Voice Is Sharp Or Flat

Although even the best singers may have occasional, temporary difficulties, intonation is a chronic problem with some singers. One singer may have a tendency to sing flat, another may tend to sing sharp, and some singers are just generally out of tune wobbling about or singing above or below the pitch in various parts of a phrase.

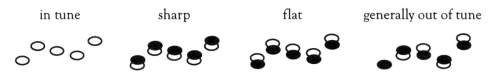

Even though singers may realize they are out of tune, they may not be able to determine whether they are sharp or flat. With a novice choir, the conductor should tell the singers whether they are sharp or flat until they are able to recognize the difference. Descriptive words sometimes help identify the problem.

	Generally Out-of-Tune	*Flat*	*Sharp*
Sounds:	fuzzy, sour or unstable	depressing, sagging or sad	harsh, nervous or tense

■ **Strategy for singers:** *To identify sharp and flat tuning, practice comparing the tuning of repeated pitches.*

■ **Activities for singers:**

1. Try to match the tuning of the second and third pitches with the first pitch.

It is important that singers learn to:
- Hear any difference in pitch.
- Identify whether a pitch is sharp or flat.
- Sing identical pitches more accurately.

This is a good exercise for **all** singers. Beginners can match the pitch before they forget the tuning of the first note. However, even experienced singers may have some difficulty with this exercise because their tuning may not be as accurate as they think it is.

2. Try to keep the tuning of the second and third pitches of each grouping matched perfectly with the first pitch.

With these two exercises, there may be a number of reasons for poor intonation. At this early stage, the singers should be encouraged to identify out-of-tune notes and adjust the tuning to match pitches. The causes should be ignored; they can be addressed later.

■ **Strategy:** *Practice tuning unison notes with other singers.*
This prepares singers for training in harmonic tuning.

■ **Activity:**

Using four to six singers at a time, tune a unison pitch:

    a) Play the pitch on the piano.

    b) Have the singers sing the pitch together for four slow beats.

    c) Stop and quickly determine which voice is sharp or flat. Those who are not singing may wish to make this judgment. Sometimes it is easier to react to criticism if the focus is on the voice, not the person. The person then feels that she has control over the voice and can correct the problem: e.g. "Julie's *voice* is a bit sharp" instead of "*Julie* is a bit sharp."

    d) Repeat a) and b). The out-of-tune singer must settle the pitch into a comfortable position with the singers who are in tune.

    e) Repeat this activity with another small group of singers using a different pitch.

Keeping the Volume Down

Most singers sing more loudly when they hear poor tuning. In their eagerness to correct an intonation problem, they increase the dynamics. This complicates the problem and may cause the music to go further out of tune. *When music is out of tune, all singers should remind themselves to sing more softly temporarily.* They will listen more carefully and each voice can be heard more easily. As a result:

- The out-of-tune voices can be identified more easily;
- It is easier to determine whether a voice is sharp or flat;
- Singers can tune more easily to other choral parts and the accompaniment because they can hear them.

Creating a Supportive Atmosphere

Singers often feel demoralized and frustrated when they realize they are out of tune. A conductor can begin to panic at the mere thought of such an ugly sound. A calm, patient approach for long-term problems works best. For short-term problems:

    1. Comment briefly on the specific problem in an unemotional manner;

    2. Give the singers an opportunity to correct the problem;

    3. Acknowledge any success.

If the attempt is not successful, the conductor can offer reassurance that the intonation will be corrected later. Sometimes success may not occur until a later rehearsal because there is not enough time currently or the conductor is unable to determine a good strategy quickly.

IV. Intonation and Repertoire

To develop good tuning, it is essential to work with repertoire that is of the highest quality. Well-crafted music with singable lyrics is easier to tune.

Poorly Chosen Lyrics

Some words are difficult to sing in tune because a vowel (e.g. "i") or consonant (e.g. "n") may encourage the throat or the mouth to close down: *walkin'*. The effect is magnified if the syllable containing the problem letter is sustained. Some initial consonants (e.g. "l, m, w") and diphthongs can encourage the voice to swoop toward the pitch: *I love listenin' by my window*.

Too many short vowels make a phrase very difficult to tune: *With every bit of sadness*.

With good lyrics, the sounds of the words have a natural beauty suited to singing; the tone quality and the tuning can be more easily controlled by the singer. Some music is a delight to sing because the words flow naturally out of the mouth. It is better to avoid music with too many difficult words. The amount of time needed to correct intonation problems with poorly crafted lyrics cannot be justified.

Poorly Crafted Music

Problems in the craft of a composition can not only make it difficult for singers to achieve good intonation but can actually lead them to be careless with tuning. The following situations can create problems with intonation:

- Awkward intervals.
- Rhythms that work against the natural emphasis of the syllables within each word.
- Melodies that work against the spoken pitch inflection of the words.
- Vowels that are difficult to tune on high pitches or sustained notes (e.g. "i" as in "hit").
- Melodies that always hover around the same pitch, encouraging singers to let the pitch "float" a bit up and down.

There is so much good music available that there is no need to include poorly crafted music. Some well-crafted pieces by well-known composers are difficult to tune. However, as long as the goal is reasonably attainable, the work on the intonation is time well spent because the final results are pleasing and the singers have learned to hone their intonation skills at a higher level.

Inappropriate Key Signatures

Sometimes a choir sings much better in tune if they perform a piece a semitone higher or lower than written. If a choir keeps going out of tune (or key) because it is gravitating to a more comfortable level, the original key may be slightly too high or low. Some conductors believe that choirs tend to sing flat in flat key signatures. If a choir is consistently flat (or sharp) with a particular piece, it is worth trying a different key.

V. Hearing Your Own Voice

Some singers have difficulty with intonation because they cannot hear their own voices while singing with a choir.

■ **Strategy:** *Give the singers opportunities to hear the true sound of their voices by using "elephant" ears.*

■ **Activity for singers:**
Use "elephant" ears during rehearsal when experiencing temporary difficulty with intonation:

Extend the size of the ears by cupping the hands behind the ears and pressing the ears very slightly forward.

These extended ears catch the sound of the true voice conducted through the air. The sound is easy to hear because it is magnified by the concave shape of the ears/hands. After achieving good tuning with the "elephant" ears, duplicate the tuning with the hands down.

■ **Strategy:** *Have the singers listen to their voices as they are reflected from a corner.*

■ **Activity for singers:**
When practicing individually, sing toward a bare corner of the room to hear the true voice reflected back.

■ **Strategy:** *Have the singers practice concentrating on the physical sensation of the pitch rather than listening to the pitch.*
A singer feels vibrations in the head or upper torso when singing. The location of the sensation varies depending on whether the pitch is high or low.

When the sopranos are singing the same pitch, they experience a physical sensation of vibrations in the same general area of their heads. However, the specific feeling varies slightly from singer to singer. For the same pitch, altos will experience the sensation in a different general area of their heads.

Because each singer experiences the physical sensation slightly differently, it is better if the conductor does not give a specific description of what they "should" be feeling, e.g. a non-specific suggestion: "Notice how the vibrations feel in your head as you sing this pitch."

■ **Activity:**

Have the singers:

a) Sing a sustained chord or a harmonic passage from the repertoire.

b) Notice the physical sensation of vibration in the body while singing.

Have one section:

a) Sing slightly out of tune with the rest of the chord.

b) Notice the physical sensation when singing out of tune.
c) Sing in tune.
d) Notice the sensation when a chord is well tuned.

In the middle of a large SATB choir, some singers cannot really hear their own voices clearly but they can feel the sensation of the pitch in their heads. Some singers learn to tune by the sensation of the physical vibrations rather than by the actual sound of the voice. When they are out of tune, the vibrations do not "feel" right. When the pitch fits well with those around it, the sensation is pleasant.

NOTE: Some singers have a habit of closing one or both ears with their hands to hear their own voices. Unfortunately, this does not help them hear the true sound in the way that others hear it projected through the air. The sound they hear inside their heads has been conducted through the bones of the head rather than through the air. During the journey from the throat to the ears, the vibrations become distorted and the quality of tone and the intonation are altered. Placing a hand over an ear also encourages singers to keep the vocal placement at the back of the head (close to the ears) rather than at the front of the mouth. When the vocal placement is back, the pitch tends to be flat. Singers should be discouraged from covering their ears.

VI. Unison and Polyphonic Music

Singers think "horizontal" as they sing unison or polyphonic music. They listen mainly to the way their own melody unfolds horizontally along the staff. They can keep in tune by comparing the tuning of later pitches with earlier pitches.

The most important pitches for tuning purposes are the tonic and the dominant because:

- They are the strongest pitches and can be heard most easily.
- They appear frequently, which makes it easier for the singer to remember the tuning of the pitches.
- If the tonic stays in tune, the singers will not drift into a higher or lower key.

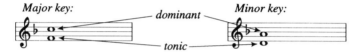

■ **Strategy:** *Teach the singers to memorize the tuning of the tonic pitch and then the dominant pitch. Together these two pitches can be used as a framework for the other pitches. When the tonic and dominant are in tune it is easier to tune the other pitches.*

■ **Activities for singers:**

1. a) Concentrate on tuning the tonic pitch exactly the same throughout one page of music.
   b) Then repeat and concentrate on tuning the dominant.

As these two pitches improve, it is amazing how quickly the tuning of the other pitches also improve.

2. With a phrase that is difficult to tune, circle the framework pitches as a reminder to focus the tuning.

3. Listen to the piano as it reinforces the tonic each time it is sung.

4. a) As you imagine the whole phrase, sing only the framework pitches aloud.

b) Sing all the pitches aloud. Make the framework pitches louder than the other pitches.

■ **Strategy:** *Teach the singers to listen for the function of the pitches within the framework.*

■ **Activities for singers:**

1. Sing a series of triads, listening carefully to the **mediant** (3rd degree):
   a) in a major key.
   b) in the minor key.
   c) in the major key again.
   d) in the major key when the mediant is slightly flat.

Because there is such a small difference in the pitch of the mediant in major and minor keys, the tonality may sound minor if the mediant is not high enough in a major key.

2. Sing a phrase with a **leading tone** moving to the tonic.

a) Repeat the phrase with a slightly flat leading tone.
b) Repeat the phrase with the leading tone high enough that it definitely leads to the tonic. Notice that the tonic now sounds more important and more satisfying.

■ **Strategy:** *Some intervals are easier to tune if the singers are aware of the chord associated with the interval.*

■ **Activity for singers:**

To sing the interval of a seventh in tune, first sing each pitch of a seventh chord.

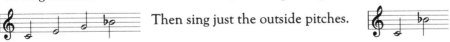

Then sing just the outside pitches.

■ **Strategy:** *Focus the pitch for melodic intervals of a semitone so that each pitch will sound distinct from its neighboring pitch.*

■ **Activity for singers:**

Imagine using a small laser beam to focus on each pitch and sing:

semitones within the scale   *chromatic pitches*

VII. Harmonic Music

When a piece of music is based on harmony, singers must think "vertically" to tune their individual pitches with the harmony sung by the choir or played in the accompaniment. Each pitch must be compared with the other pitches in the chord for accurate tuning.

There are two ways to tune harmonically based music:
1) harmonizing with the chord: fitting a pitch with the rest of the chord
2) balancing with another line: one part steadies its tuning with another part as the parts move in opposite directions

Harmonizing

When two (or more) parts move generally in the same direction, the singers must fit the pitches together comfortably.

■ **Strategy:** *Think of the parts fitting together as a duet.*

■ **Activity for singers:**
Know which parts move together with the same general pitch contour. Rehearse those parts separately so that everyone can hear how the tuning fits together.

excerpt from *O Süsser Mai* by Johannes Brahms [Kjos 8739]

Then add the other part.

Balancing
SATB Choirs
In most harmonically based music, the bass and soprano are very important for tuning because the melody (often sung by the sopranos) and the bass line usually act as a framework for the inner parts. This tradition comes from the Baroque period when the sopranos often had the chorale melody and a strong bass line was used to outline the harmonies. The tuning of the bass and soprano parts should be secured first and then the other parts can fit their tuning within this framework.

The soprano and bass parts often move in contrary motion. The sopranos can balance their tuning with the basses as the two parts move in opposite directions (as the basses can balance their tuning with the sopranos). In this way the framework tends not to go sharp (towards the sopranos) or flat (towards the basses).

■ **Strategy:** *For harmonically based music, first isolate the outer parts to display those pitches clearly and to let the two parts balance the tuning with each other. Then the inner parts can tune within the framework of the outer parts.*

■ **Activities:**
1. a) Take a short section of music, such as this excerpt from Bach's Cantata 140, *Wachet Auf* and have the basses and sopranos sing their parts together.

excerpt from Gloria Sei Dir by J.S. Bach [Kjos 8746]

   b) Repeat with the basses and sopranos facing each other, and listening to each other to balance the pitch. With some practice, the pitch will become more stable.

   c) Add the altos and tenors. They should listen carefully to the outer parts to fit their pitches within the framework.

2. It is easier to tune the inner parts when the outer parts can be clearly heard. Have the sopranos and basses stand while the altos and tenors remain seated. Because of this position, the sopranos and basses:
   • will sing more loudly;
   • can be heard more easily because their heads are higher than the other singers.

Children's Choirs

Children should start singing in parts (e.g. rounds, easy harmonic singing) as early as possible. Many children do not learn to sing in tune until they have experiences with harmony.

Even in unison singing, children can be directed to listen to the accompaniment (as they sing) to balance the unison line with the lower pitches in the piano accompaniment. This gives the children some experience with harmony.

In children's part singing, the outer two parts create a harmonic framework (e.g. the first soprano and alto in unaccompanied SSA music). The tuning of the outer parts should be secured first and then the inner part can fit the tuning within that framework.

■ **Strategy:** *Harmonize by listening carefully to the other parts.*
■ **Activity:**
Have one side of the choir face the other (or the front of the choir face the back) so that all the singers are encouraged to listen more carefully to the other part(s).

If the children have difficulty with this activity, have them sing one phrase while concentrating on listening to the other part, and then sing the next phrase while concentrating on listening just to their own part. Gradually increase their stamina to sing one part and listen to another at the same time.

■ **Strategy:** *Balance the tuning with the lower pitches in the piano accompaniment.*
■ **Activity:**
Have the accompanist emphasize the bass line of the accompaniment or play it in octaves while the singers listen without singing:

excerpt from *Agnus Dei* by W.A. Mozart [Kjos 8736]

Then have the singers sing their part(s) with the piano accompaniment, while focusing on listening to the bass line and balancing their pitches with it.

Key Changes
■ **Strategy:** *When the music changes key, stabilize the new key by clarifying the new tonic pitch before adding the other parts.*

■ **Activities:**
1. With a rapid key change:
   a) If one part sings the same pitch which is in the last chord of the old key and the first chord of the new key, practice that part alone first.
   b) Add the part that moves to the new tonic. If the singers have sung this pitch in the previous phrase, they can memorize the pitch as they sing it.
   c) Add the other parts quietly at first so that they can hear the new tonic clearly and tune with it. A slower tempo may help.
   d) Repeat more loudly.

excerpt from *Celebration* by Nancy Telfer [Kjos 8743]

2. With a gradual key modulation:
   a) As a general rule: If a pitch is repeated from one chord to the next, sing the repeated note louder. All other pitches should be sung more softly and tuned with the repeated pitch.
   b) When a phrase moves toward a new chord, use separate practice for the part singing the pitch that determines the new chord.

excerpt from *There Shall a Star* by Felix Mendelssohn [Kjos 8773]

determining pitch
(usually an accidental)

i) Sing the phrase, pausing on the determining pitch.

ii) Repeat the measures with the other singers singing softly, retaining the pause to clarify the new chord.

iii) Repeat again at the usual tempo.

c) When the music moves quickly through several keys, practice the easiest choral part first and then tune the other parts with it.

Sectional Problems

Sometimes only one vocal part is out of tune. The singers on that part need to identify the problem pitches and practice tuning them. This cannot be effectively achieved in a sectional rehearsal. The singers need to hear the full choir around them to improve the harmonic tuning.

■ **Strategy:** *Give the out-of-tune singers an opportunity to hear the other parts more clearly.*

■ **Activities:**

1. Have the singers on the out-of-tune part sing more softly while the others sing with moderate dynamics.

2. Use a slower tempo as the singers concentrate on the harmony around them to determine which of their own pitches are out of tune.

■ **Strategy for singers:** *Mark the chronically out-of-tune pitches as a reminder.*

■ **Activity for singers:**

Quickly circle out-of-tune pitches. Then:

a) Sing the passage, pausing on each problem chord to tune the problem pitch with the other pitches in the chord.

b) Repeat, tuning the problem pitch more quickly.

c) Repeat, tuning the problem pitch immediately.

d) Resume the usual tempo.

Close Harmony

When the pitches of a chord are very close together, they act like magnets. It is easy for one pitch to be "persuaded" to move closer to another and then the integrity of the tuning is lost.

■ **Strategy for singers:** *Focus the pitch for close harmony so that each pitch will be clearly defined beside any neighboring pitches.*

■ **Activity for singers:**

Imagine using a small laser beam to focus on each pitch when there are close pitches within a chord or tone cluster.

VIII. Help for Choirs With Multiple Tuning Problems

Sometimes multiple tuning problems exist within a choir: some singers' voices are flat, others are sharp, and the intonation may fluctuate with the remaining singers. Multiple tuning problems are greatly reduced when a choir tunes unison music by comparing recurring tonic and dominant pitches (see Chapter VI) and when they tune harmonic music by harmonizing and balancing the outer choral parts against each other (see Chapter VII). The following ideas are also useful for addressing multiple tuning problems.

Keeping the Ears Fresh

When the ears are fresh, they can identify intonation problems much more easily. With some thoughtful planning, conductors can minimize listening fatigue, a problem that develops very quickly when singers become overloaded with unpleasant sounds of out-of-tune singing.

- ■ **Strategy:** *Pace the rehearsal so that the singers do not sing music that is difficult to tune for extended periods of time.*
- ■ **Activities:**
  1. Alternate challenging music with music that the singers can tune fairly well.

  2. Alternate a moment's silence with a few moments of work on the tuning. The silence gives the ears a rest so that they can work more efficiently.

  3. Alternate work on tuning with work that uses the brain or the emotions instead of the ears:
     a) Memorization (one or two lines at a time);
     b) An explanation of the lyrics;
     c) Speaking a few lines of the lyrics emotively, etc.

- ■ **Strategy:** *Simplify complex music until the tuning has stabilized.*
- ■ **Activities:**
  1. Simplify complicated accompaniments so that the ears are not overloaded with sound. Sometimes it is best just to play a rhythmic framework on the piano (e.g. the first chord of each bar). When the tuning has stabilized, resume the use of the original accompaniment.

excerpt from *There Shall a Star* by Felix Mendelssohn [Kjos 8773]

2. Do not add other instrumental parts (e.g. percussion, flute, etc.) until the tuning has stabilized.

■ **Strategy:** *Move the position of the singers so that:*
    a) they will be able to hear each other more easily;
    b) the novelty of the new formation will encourage them to listen more carefully.

■ **Activity:**
Rehearse the music for one piece in any of the following formations:
- Each side of the choir facing toward the center;
- A large circle;
- A double circle (one circle inside the other);
- Small groups of three or four singers with space between each group.

Rehearsing Music With "U" ("oo" as in soon)
"U" is the softest vowel. With this vowel, the singers are able to hear their own and other voices better.

"U" is also the most focused vowel. Because the pitch is more definite when it is focused, it is easier to hear clearly and it is easier to tell whether it matches the tuning of another pitch.

"U" has a natural forward placement. This also helps the tuning. If the placement is too far back, the tuning tends to be flat.

■ **Strategy:** *Rehearse sections of repertoire with the "u" vowel to identify out-of-tune pitches and to focus the tuning.*

■ **Activity for singers:**
    a) Sing a short section of the music to "u," listening carefully to the intonation.

excerpt from Coventry Carol arranged by Nancy Telfer [Kjos 6256]

    b) Repeat with the lyrics, trying to keep the tone as well focused as it was with the "u."

    c) Alternate phrases between "u" and the lyrics, always maintaining the focus during the lyrics.

Using the Circle Concept

Many singers sound out of tune because of poor tone quality. In some cases the fundamental tone of each pitch may be in tune but the singers may sound flat (or sharp) because all the overtones needed for each pitch are not vibrating. When only the high, bright overtones are in use, the pitch will be sharp; with only lower overtones, the pitch will sound flat.

The shape of the mouth cavity determines which overtones and what quantity of each is activated for each pitch. In private lessons a singer can learn exactly how to shape this cavity to achieve a good quality of tone and good intonation. It is not possible for a choral conductor to give individual instructions for each choir member and it is not necessary for choral singers to know about overtones. However, if the singers simply imagine a full circle of sound as they sing, they can begin to experience the benefits of all the desirable overtones balanced nicely together for good tuning.

As the singers see the full circle in their minds, the overtones tend to automatically fall into place and the tuning tends to improve immediately. Both flat and sharp singing tend to settle into the center of the pitch. If the singers were to imagine a straight line, the pitch would be flat. A triangle would make the pitch sharp. A full circle creates a sensation that includes the use of all the important overtones.

The image of a full circle is particularly useful in choirs when there are multiple causes for intonation problems. In a choir of forty singers there may be forty different causes of poor intonation in a particular piece. Over a long period of time it may be important to address each of these problems but, in one rehearsal, this would be far too time consuming. The image of a circle may be able to correct most or all of these problems in a few seconds.

■ **Strategy for singers:** *While singing, imagine a circle of sound to center the pitch.*
■ **Activity for singers:**
    a) Sing a phrase, imagining that a voice produces a circle of sound that pours forward out of the mouth in the shape of a tube.
    b) Repeat, imagining that the sound is filling only the bottom half of the circle. Notice how flat the pitch is.

    c) Repeat, imagining that the sound is filling only the top half of the circle. Notice how sharp the pitch is.

    d) Repeat, imagining a full circle in tune.

NOTE: Whenever the tuning is poor in rehearsal, remind the singers about the circle image. Once the singers have worked with the concept of a circle, they can quickly duplicate the sensation whenever it is needed.

Staccato For Experienced Singers

Experienced singers at any age can have multiple tuning problems. This frequently happens when teenage singers are going through a vocal growth spurt or adult singers' voices are suddenly being reshaped by new information about vocal production. The good news in these situations is that the tone quality of the voices is rapidly improving. The bad news is that there is temporary difficulty (sometimes severe difficulty) with intonation.

Any of the strategies mentioned in this book may be of help in these situations but in some repertoire with advanced singers, it may be helpful to rehearse a short legato section with staccato articulation. Because poor tuning is more obvious when the pitches are very short, the singers can identify individual problems more easily. Because each note has such short duration, each pitch must be tuned immediately. The singer provides more controlled support for the tuning because staccato technique requires more concentration.

With novice singers, staccato rehearsal should be avoided so that the undeveloped voices are not stressed.

■ **Strategy for experienced singers:** *Practice legato passages with staccato articulation to focus the tuning.*

■ **Activity for experienced singers:**

    a) Sing through a short section with legato articulation.

excerpt from *Je Ne Fus Jamais Si Aise* by Pierre Certon [Kjos 5757]

Du — du — du   du   du du du du   du du du du du   du du du

    b) Repeat, using staccato articulation on all notes.

Du du du du du   du   du du du du   du du du du du   du du du

    c) Repeat, bringing each staccato pitch into tune more quickly.

    d) Repeat with legato phrasing, keeping the focus on the intonation.

IX. Flat Singing: Problems With Vocal Production

Listening skills are very important. However, a singer may be a good listener but may still sing flat because the poor tuning is caused by poor vocal production. This can be very frustrating for the singer who is intensely aware of the problem but cannot seem to correct it. No matter how good the listening skills are, a singer will not sing in tune until the vocal production problems are corrected.

A number of common problems with vocal production that can cause flat singing include:

- Inadequate air pressure;
- A lack of vocal energy;
- Failure of the soft palate to lift properly;
- Vocal placement too far back or too low in the mouth;
- Chronic tension;
- Mouth not open enough;
- Lack of resonance.

Air Pressure

Without consistent, steady pressure in the flow of air, the pitch can sag. First, the singers must learn to inhale enough air to maintain pressure throughout a phrase.

■ **Strategy:** *Expand the lung capacity so that there is enough air to support the pitch.*

■ **Activity for singers:**
  a) Inhale slowly for four beats to partially fill the lungs.
  b) Maintain the inner pressure for four beats.
  c) Continue to inhale for four more beats, completely filling the lungs.
  d) Release the air for eight beats.
   inhale: 1 2 3 4
   maintain pressure: 1 2 3 4
   continue inhaling: 1 2 3 4
   release: 1 2 3 4 5 6 7 8

  e) Shorten the time for inhalation:
   inhale: 1 2
   maintain pressure: 1 2
   continue inhaling: 1 2
   release: 1 2 3 4 5 6 7 8

  f) Fill up the lungs in one beat:
   inhale: 1
   release: 1 2 3 4 5 6 7 8

By gradually shortening the time for inhalation, the exercise becomes more realistic: there is often not much time to inhale between phrases.

Some singers may have developed good inhalation techniques but may not have worked on developing steady air pressure for the release of the air.

■ **Strategy for singers:** *Apply more air pressure in situations where the pitch tends to go flat.*

■ **Activity for singers:**

    a) Sing a descending scale, starting with steady air pressure but using less pressure for the last few notes. Notice the tendency to go flat on the lower pitches.

    b) Repeat the scale, starting with steady air pressure but increasing the pressure for the last few notes. Let the pressure help keep the lower pitches in tune.

Many singers' low pitches are often flat or unsteady because they do not use enough air pressure.

■ **Strategy for singers:** *Build breath control quickly by exercising the necessary abdominal muscles.*

■ **Activity for singers:**

    a) Hiss the rhythms of a familiar phrase:

    b) Repeat, noticing how much pressure is needed to articulate each part of the phrase.

    c) Sing with the lyrics, maintaining the same quality of pressure.

excerpt from *Laudate Dominum* by W.A. Mozart [Kjos 8731]

Vocal Energy

If the tone lacks energy, the pitch tends to become flat. This is a common problem with sustained notes and slow music. In rhythmic music, the articulation of the rhythms gives a momentum to the energy which can keep the pitch from becoming flat. With a sustained note, the beginning articulation may contribute enough energy to start the note in tune. However, without the help of additional articulations, the pitch may start to sink. If the singer continually feeds the sound with a little energy, it is easier to keep the pitch steady.

■ **Strategy for singers:** *Keep the energy constantly alive on longer notes to keep the pitch from sinking.*

■ **Activity for singers:**
Sing a descending scale, imagining that the sound is spinning forward through the air in the form of a ball.

When an object (e.g. a top) is spinning, it may "sing" a pitch. As the object gradually moves more slowly, the pitch winds downwards. As the singers imagine a steady spinning sensation, the pitch keeps up. The momentum of the movement keeps the voice placement forward.

Raised Soft Palate

At the back of the top of the mouth is a small flap of soft tissue, the soft palate, which should be up when singing. If it is not up, the pitch tends to be flat. Some singers are flat all the time because the soft palate is not raised. Other singers close down the soft palate because they are worried or tense (e.g. while singing a high pitch) and become flat just for that pitch.

Singers can feel the soft palate move when they yawn. When the soft palate is raised, the cavity inside the mouth is much larger and the soft palate tissue does not dampen the sound. With the soft palate in the correct position, a greater variety of overtones can be effectively produced to place each pitch in tune.

If the singers concentrate too much on the soft palate, they tend to let the vocal placement go into the back of the throat. Therefore, it is better to avoid talking about the soft palate too much in group singing. Indirect activities can be used to raise the soft palate.

32

- **Strategy for singers:** *Use a visual image which will cause the soft palate to lift.*
- **Activities for singers:**

  1. a) Form one hand into an inverted "U" in front of the face and then sing a descending scale. The soft palate is extremely susceptible to visual suggestion. It automatically tries to imitate the position of the hand by changing from its usual rather flat position to an arched (raised) position.

    b) Repeat, starting without the hand and adding the hand in an inverted "U" in the middle of the scale. Notice how much easier it is to keep the pitch from going flat in the second half of the scale.

    c) Repeat, starting with the hand in an inverted "U" and then forming a flat, horizontal position with the hand in the middle of the scale. Notice how the pitch flattens as the hand flattens.

    d) Repeat, using the inverted "U" throughout the scale. Memorize the physical sensation of singing this way. The correct position of the soft palate may not be sustained for too long at first. It takes some time to develop stamina.

  2. During a rehearsal piece:

    a) Form an inverted "U" with one hand at the side of the head. Memorize the physical sensation inside the mouth.

    b) Repeat without the hand but try to duplicate the physical sensation present with the "U."

    c) Alternate with and without the hand until the physical sensation can be duplicated without it.

Voice Placement
If the vocal placement is too far back in the head, the pitch tends to be flat.

■ **Strategy for singers:** *Use a physical gesture to experience forward vocal placement.*
■ **Activity for singers:**
    a) Place the hands at the sides of the face with palms facing inwards.

    b) Sing a phrase while moving the hands slowly forward.

excerpt from Laudate Dominum by W.A. Mozart [Kjos 8731]

    c) Repeat without using the hands but imagining the hand movement.

    d) Alternate phrases with and without hands, trying to keep the voice forward without using the hands.

This activity is very powerful because the singer's own hands are telling the voice what to do. If singers memorize the sensation of forward placement as they use the hands, they can duplicate the sensation when the hands are no longer used.

    Some singers normally center their voices a bit too low in the mouth. This changes the shape of the cavity within the mouth and the sound does not exit cleanly from the throat out through the mouth. As a result, the pitch tends to be flat. Although this is a chronic problem for a few singers, many other singers just place the voice low in the mouth on lower pitches.

■ **Strategy for singers:** *Keep the pitch focused high enough in the mouth.*
■ **Activities for singers:**
   1. a) Sing a descending scale.

   b) Repeat, showing a bit more of the front top teeth. Notice how much easier
      it is to keep the pitch from going flat.

2. On a low-pitched phrase in rehearsal music, show a bit more of the top front
teeth.

Because the singers are concentrating on the top teeth, the tone will focus a bit
higher in the mouth. When a singer raises the upper lip to show more of the top
teeth, the dampening effect of the lip is removed. Because the teeth are hard,
they tend to resonate more with the brighter overtones if the upper lip is not
dampening these overtones. The result of all these changes is that the pitch tends
to lose its flatness.

Chronic Tension

If a singer is frequently flat and has difficulty correcting this tuning problem, he or
she may be chronically tense. Tension can cause rigidity in the vocal mechanism.
When the natural flexibility is no longer present, the pitch can become locked in at
a lower (or higher) level.

   Physical and psychological freedom can release the singers from chronic vocal
tension. It may take weeks or months for a singer to become more relaxed but the
rewards are great.

   The physical environment of the singers should be conducive to relaxation:
   1. A comfortable temperature makes quite a difference during a rehearsal. If
      the temperature is too hot, the tension slowly rises. If it is too cold, the
      muscles quickly become tense.
   2. Non-restrictive clothing, particularly about the throat and waist, help to
      relax the singers.
   3. Appropriate footwear is important. When the feet are tense, the whole
      body tends to be tense.
   4. There should be some space between the singers because overcrowding
      can also create tension.

The singers should also have a relaxed psychological environment. This is discussed
in Chapter X.

Shyness

When singers are shy, they may have a tendency to sing flat. They are "hiding" from the world around them by:
- Keeping their mouths partially closed;
- Letting their posture sag;
- Keeping their eyes pointed down.

When singers have their eyes raised toward the conductor, the pitch tends to keep up. When the eyes are almost closed, the opening of the mouth tends to be almost closed and the soft palate tends to be down. As soon as the eyes move up, the mouth opens more and sometimes the soft palate rises, too.

■ **Strategy for singers:** *Become aware of the importance of the eye position.*
■ **Activity for singers:**
   a) Sing a descending scale with eyes pointing down.

   b) Repeat with eyes toward the conductor. Notice that the pitch tends to keep better in tune.

■ **Strategy for singers:** *Look at the conductor's eyes as much as possible. When the eyes are on the conductor, the tuning is better.*

NOTE: Some singers become shy only during a concert. In the pre-concert rehearsals, it is important to train the singers to keep their eyes directed toward the conductor's eyes as much as possible.

■ **Activities for conductors:**
   1. During rehearsals, do some unexpected things with your conducting (e.g. a tempo change, unexpected dynamics, etc.) so that the singers feel that unless they watch the conductor they will be exposed.

   2. Move away from the conducting stand to other parts of the room. The singers must follow you with their eyes.

   3. Warn the singers that anything can happen in the concert and that this is one of the exciting aspects of performance. If the singers watch the conductor, then the ensemble is free to do something quite remarkable that may not have happened before.

The physical position of the eyes helps the tuning but there is also a benefit created by clearing the pathway from the conductor through the eyes of the singers to the emotional intelligence of the brain. When the singers are watching the conductor during the performance, the singers tend to react to the appearance of the conductor. They subconsciously imitate the conductor in some way. They can forget their shyness when they become involved with the confidence projected by the conductor or as they shape the mood of the music with the help of the conductor's gestures or facial expressions. The conductor is hearing an "ideal" performance of the music within his or her mind and that is reflected in everything the conductor does. If the singers are watching, the conductor can project this "ideal" sound right into the heart of the entire ensemble.

Resonance

When a singer has good resonance, appropriate overtones for each pitch vibrate. Without some of the higher overtones, the pitch can sound flat.

■ **Strategy for singers:** *Activate the higher overtones through the use of humming and glides.*

■ **Activities for singers:**

1. Do some humming in the middle of the range as part of the warmup.

Humming creates more vibrations than singing vowels. Humming in midrange activates high-pitched overtones. When these high-pitched overtones are warmed up, pitches in all parts of the range tend to be more in tune.

2. a) Hum a passage that tends to be flat, keeping the focus of the hum in the upper lip.

b) Repeat with the lyrics, using the same amount of resonance created with the humming.

excerpt from *Cast Your Burden Upon the Lord* by Felix Mendelssohn [Kjos 8738]

Some singers hum flat. When the hum is focused in the upper lip, the pitch is higher.

3. As a warmup, have the singers practice slow glides:

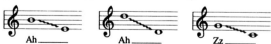

If the tempo is slow enough, all the pitches between the chromatic pitches will be sung, activating more overtones. When these overtones are warmed up, it is easier to use them while singing repertoire.

X. Sharp Singing

The most common cause of sharp singing is a tight throat. When a violin string is tightened, the pitch of the violin rises. When a throat becomes tighter, the pitch of the voice rises. When the area around the throat and mouth is relaxed, the singer can control the pitch more easily.

Some singers are generally tense, with the source of tension rooted in a particular part of the body. Because the tension can begin in one area and then spread to the mouth and throat, a singer must learn to become aware of the state of relaxation throughout the body. Singers can minimize tension by:

- Consistently using good posture while singing;
- Keeping the knees slightly flexed;
- Relaxing the muscles with large, slow physical movements during warmups and breaks;
- Changing the position of the body whenever possible (i.e. during rests or interludes);
- Imagining relaxing images to promote a relaxed frame of mind.

Information on general chronic tension can be found in Chapter IX. A discussion of specific areas of tension follows.

Tension In the Tongue

Some people try to control their lives with their tongues. Their tongues are constantly pushing and searching. If the tongue becomes tense:

- The tissue in the tongue feels tougher and the sides of the vocal tract become harder. Hard surfaces bring out the brighter overtones and the pitch tends to become sharp.
- The throat becomes tense because the back of the tongue is connected with the throat. Any tension in the tongue is quickly transferred to the throat.

The tongue should be flat and relaxed to prevent sharp singing. If a singer thinks about the tongue too much, it may start to become tense. Any activities with the tongue should be short in duration and then the attention should be directed to another topic.

■ **Strategy:** *Force the tongue to become so tense that it must react by relaxing.*
■ **Activity for singers:**
   a) Draw a simple picture with the tip of the tongue in the air.

b) Let the tongue return to the singing position: the tip of the tongue should touch the spot where the bottom front teeth meet the gums; the tongue should lie thin and flat.

NOTE: The tongue is relatively tense or firm while it draws, but it automatically tends to relax immediately afterwards. The stronger the tension, the more relaxed the reaction is.

■ **Strategy for singers:** *Use a mind image to create a relaxed sensation in the tongue.*
■ **Activity for singers:**
  a) Imagine that he or she is cradling a plum within the mouth for a moment.
  b) Wiggle the tongue.
  c) Repeat the image, noticing how thin the tongue feels.
  d) Wiggle the tongue.
  e) Sing a short legato phrase keeping the image in the mind.
  f) Rest for two bars.
  g) Repeat the same phrase.

(plum)

Tension In the Chin
If the chin is tight, the throat is tight. If the chin points forward or upward, the throat is stretched and tense.

■ **Strategy for singers:** *Create some tension in the jaw and then let gravity help the jaw relax.*
■ **Activity for singers:**
Have each singer do the following motions:
  a) Keeping the mouth closed, slowly move the chin down to touch the chest.
  b) Gradually let the chin rise to a level position. Notice the tendency of the jaw to relax downwards with the help of gravity.
  c) Repeat the activity. When the jaw relaxes, let it fall open.

■ **Strategy for singers:** *Loosen the jaw by slowly exercising the jaw muscles.*
■ **Activity for singers:**
  a) Imagine that there is a big wad of bubble gum in your mouth.
  b) Use slow, chewing motions to loosen the jaw.

Tension In the Shoulders

When the shoulders are relaxed and down, it is easier to keep the throat relaxed. Some singers habitually use a posture where the shoulders are kept high as if to provide defensive armor for the throat.

■ **Strategy for singers:** *Use slow, continual motions to relax the shoulders.*
■ **Activity for singers:**
Slowly roll one shoulder up and forward; then perform the same motion with the other shoulder.

■ **Strategy for singers:** *Use gravity to relax the shoulders.*
■ **Activity for singers:**
a) Spread the arms out to the sides in an "airplane" position.

b) Slowly let the arms float into a bank to the right, then the left, then the right again.

c) Let gravity gradually bring the arms and shoulders down until the arms are at the sides.

d) Immediately sing a legato phrase from the choir's repertoire.

excerpt from *Benedictus* by Franz Schubert [Kjos 8730]

Be-ne - dic - tus qui ve - nit in no - mi-ne Do - mi - ni,

■ **Strategy:** *Have the singers massage the tension out of each other's shoulders.*

■ **Activity:**

Have each row in the choir face the side of the room so that each singer can massage the shoulders of the singer in front. Encourage them to use small circular motions, starting at the neck and firmly moving out toward the arms. Face the opposite side and repeat.

Tension In the Arms

If the arms are tight, the tension will spread up into the shoulders and throat. Because of excitement or nervousness, some singers may even be clenching their hands into fists. When the hands clench, the throat also clenches.

Some singers maintain a singing position with their folders throughout a rehearsal; when they lock their arms into place for such an extended period of time, incredible tension is created. The longer they stay in the same position, the tenser the arms become.

■ **Strategy for singers:** *Temporarily increase the arm tension as much as possible so that the muscles will react by relaxing.*

■ **Activity for singers:**

   a) Make a tight fist with both hands and hold for a few seconds.

   b) Relax the hands. Notice that the throat quickly relaxes as the hands relax.

   c) Sing a sustained high pitch, keeping the throat relaxed. Stop singing before tension creeps in again. This technique can be used during a few measures of rest in rehearsal or during a concert.

■ **Strategy for singers:** *Hold the folder (or music) so that:*
   • *The head will be in a good position for singing;*
   • *The arms will be as comfortable as possible.*

■ **Activity for singers:**

Experiment to find a comfortable way of holding the folder. Because of the different sizes of singers, each person must find a suitable position. Other singers may have helpful suggestions to share.

■ **Strategy for singers:** *To avoid building up tension in the arms, hold the folder (or music) in concert position only when necessary.*

■ **Activity for singers:**

    a) Lift the music into singing position when the conductor's arms rise into a conducting position during rehearsal or at the beginning of a concert.

    b) Move the position of the music down when not actually singing. This may be a subtle movement during a concert but in rehearsal singers may temporarily place the music on their laps while listening to longer interludes or soloists. When the conductor's arms drop to the sides, this is a sign that the singers will not need to sing right away. The singers' arms should also go down.

General Body Tension

It is often helpful to use slow physical movements to relax the entire body. These are most effective:

    • At the beginning of a rehearsal;

    • Right before a piece that tends to go sharp;

    • As a change of pace between rehearsal pieces.

■ **Strategy:** *Have the singers use large, slow body movements to create a general sense of relaxation.*

■ **Activity:**

Make enough space between singers so that everybody can move both arms in large, slow circles at the sides of the body. A large movement encourages the full body to become more involved and also encompasses the singer's mood more completely. The space between singers also helps them to relax because they feel less crowded.

■ **Strategy for singers:** *Induce relaxation through shaking motions.*

■ **Activity for singers:**

Gently shake:

    a) The right leg;

    b) The left leg;

    c) Both hands;

    d) The arms from wrists to upper arms;

    e) The shoulders.

Let the shoulders rise with the vibrations and then relax.

42

■ **Strategy for singers:** *Release the strain of gravity by letting the muscles sag upside down.*

■ **Activity for singers:**
    a) Lean the body forward from the waist, letting the upper part of the body hang down.
    b) Feel the backbone lengthen as it hangs;
    c) Gradually rise, keeping the back relaxed and leaving the head down until the last moment. When the head is no longer in a position of authority, the whole body tends to relax more.

■ **Strategy for singers:** *Use a slow, repetitive motion to calm the mind and relax the body.*

■ **Activity for singers:**
For the following exercise, move one hand in a slow circular motion parallel to the floor. The phrase may be repeated over and over again in a round.

This physical movement could also be used with slow, lyric repertoire.

■ **Strategy for singers:** *Use a mind image to simulate a relaxed experience.*

■ **Activities for singers:**
Imagine:
    a) lying on the beach;
    b) floating on a cloud;
    c) wrapping a soft towel around the body;
    d) placing smooth pebbles in a circle.

Because each mind is unique, the choice of an appropriate image is very important.

Providing a Relaxed Psychological Environment

The general atmosphere of a rehearsal should promote relaxation and well being as the singers strive for high standards. The relationship between the conductor and the singers can shape the attitude of the singers. If the conductor is polite, personable, and respectful, he or she can have very high expectations without the singers becoming tense.

Each rehearsal must be paced well so that hard work is balanced with more relaxing work. Relaxed singers have a glow about them as they sing. Too many instructions can create tension or confusion. The conductor must know when to continue with one idea and when it is time to start a new idea.

The conductor's speaking voice and the conductor's body are two main tools that help to shape the psychological environment. A pleasant speaking voice that uses some variety in pitch and pacing keeps the rehearsal relaxed and yet still stimulating. When conductors listen to a recorded rehearsal, they may be astounded to hear the way their voices sound to the singers.

Because the singers are facing the conductor, the conductor's body acts as a model and the singers tend to mirror the posture of the conductor. If a conductor's body is tense, it is difficult for the singers to relax. Some conductors can minimize the effects of a tense body by wearing loose clothing.

If the beat pattern of the conductor is fairly low, singers tend to be more relaxed. With a higher beat pattern, the singers tend to breathe more shallowly and generally be more tense in the area of the throat.

Humor is an effective tool that can be created with either the conductor's voice or body. Choir members may also contribute their own humor. When a choir is accustomed to a relaxed rehearsal with some humor, the singers arrive with the expectation of a pleasurable experience and the conductor does not need to work as hard to help the singers move through the transition from everyday life to a world of music.

Rehearsal Strategies for the Conductor:
- *Be polite, personable and respectful.*
- *Balance hard work with more relaxing activities.*
- *Do not overload the singers with instructions.*
- *Use a pleasant speaking voice.*
- *Keep your own body relaxed.*
- *Do not let the beat pattern become too high.*
- *Let humor be a part of your rehearsal.*

XI. Pronunciation and Intonation

Uniform Vowels

Although each person in a group may pronounce the same vowel differently as they speak, it is important that all singers use uniform pronunciation as they sing. Otherwise, the mixture of sounds for one single vowel can create a distortion in the intonation.

■ **Strategy:** *Help the singers become more aware of the effect of uniform vowels on the pitch.*

■ **Activity:**
Have each section of the choir sing a phrase simultaneously using a different pronunciation of the vowel "ah."

    e.g.   sopranos: a bright "ah" (focused on top, front teeth)
                altos: "aw" (low in the mouth)
                tenors: a covered "ah" (mouth partially closed)
                basses: a very dark "ah" (placement at the back of the head)

Repeat, using uniform pronunciation of "ah." Notice the clarity of the tuning.

Singers should be encouraged to use uniform vowels, not uniform tone. When they use uniform vowels, each voice will still sound unique because the timbre of each voice is different. In an orchestra, the sound of the violin section shimmers because each instrument has been constructed with slightly different materials and has a slightly different timbre. This same effect is created in a choir when voices with different timbres are singing together. The tone quality is made richer by the variety of timbres.

Rich, contrasting timbres in some choirs create an extremely vibrant sound causing some listeners to feel that the singers are not in tune while other listeners may be quite comfortable with the tuning. This discrepancy in opinion is a matter of taste that may have been established because the listener has been constantly exposed to a vibrant sound (or an extremely blended sound) and has come to believe that what they are accustomed to is a desirable quality in a choir. If a conductor wants more uniformity of timbre without sacrificing the unique quality of each voice, a different seating plan may be used. Seating plans are discussed in Chapter XXII.

Uniform Diphthongs

Diphthongs also need to be uniformly presented. When the singers know which vowels are used in the diphthong, they can practice coordinating the length of the vowel that is sustained. If some singers are on the first vowel while the others are already on the second vowel, the tuning will not be pure.

■ **Strategy for singers:** *Sing the first vowel of most diphthongs as long as possible before moving on to the second vowel.*

■ **Activity for singers:**
    a) Omit the second vowel of the diphthong: change "my" to "mah."
    b) Add the diphthong at the last possible moment: sing "mah———ee."

Vowel Color

If a vowel is too bright, it may sound sharp. If it is too dark, it may sound flat. Some people use such a bright speaking voice that it makes the people around them feel edgy. Sharp singing has the same effect on an audience: the listeners start to become uncomfortable and restless. Very dark speaking and singing voices tend to sound flat. When the vowel is neither too bright nor too dark, the tone lies in the center of the pitch.

■ **Strategy:** *Help the singers to become more aware of the effect of the color of the vowel on the pitch.*

■ **Activities for singers:**

1. Have the singers sing a phrase using a bright "ah."

   Repeat with a dark "ah." Have the singers notice the flatter pitch with the dark "ah."

2. To achieve a more uniform color, have all the singers open their mouths in a "north/south" direction rather than "east/west."
   When the mouth is open too far sideways, the tone becomes twangy and the pitch tends to be flat.

   "north/south"   "east/west"

Consonants

Crisp consonants help keep the pitch up. When a consonant is formed fairly high at the front of the mouth, it sounds crisper and the pitch of the consonant is higher. If the consonant is in tune, it is easier to sing the following vowel in tune. The energy of the initial consonant(s) also helps keep the pitch of the vowel up.

Lazy consonants tend to promote flat singing. Because they are pronounced lower in the mouth and sometimes farther back in the mouth, the pitch tends to be lower.

Most consonants should be enunciated with quick, small movements at the front of the mouth.

■ **Strategy for singers:** *Become more aware of lazy consonants.*
■ **Activity for singers:**

 a) Sing a phrase with lazy consonants; notice the affect on the intonation.

 b) Repeat the phrase with crisp consonants.

excerpt from *There Shall A Star* by Felix Mendelssohn [Kjos 8773]

The beginning consonant(s) of a syllable should be pitched at the same level as the vowel that follows. If the consonant starts at a lower level than the vowel, the pitch will swoop up to the vowel and may not actually reach the correct pitch.

 Sustained consonants (e.g. l, m, n) affect the pitch of the vowel most obviously, but consonants which are produced quickly (e. g. b, p, t) can also be initiated too low in pitch and then the voice has to move up to the pitch of the vowel. Although consonants like "s" and "f" do not have a specific pitch, they can have a relatively low pitch which can affect the following vowel.

■ **Strategy for singers:** *Sing initial consonants at the same pitch as the vowel that follows.*
■ **Activity for singers:**

 a) Start each consonant at a lower pitch and glide up to the vowel.

 b) Repeat the exercise but start each consonant on the same pitch as the vowel.

XII. Singing Soft Music

Soft music often tends to be flat. There may be several causes for this:
- A tendency to slow down the tempo;
- Problems in vocal production;
- A lack of understanding of the nature of dynamics.

Slow Tempos For Soft Music

When music suddenly becomes soft, there is a tendency to sing more slowly. With a slower tempo, it is more difficult to keep the pitch up.

■ **Strategy for singers:** *Keep the tempo moving even when dynamics suddenly become soft.*

■ **Activity for singers:**
   a) Mark the beat or pulse in the measures right before and after the change in dynamics.

excerpt from *Laudate Dominum* by W.A. Mozart [Kjos 8731]

   b) Sing the excerpt, with attention to the tempo of the inner rhythms.
   c) Repeat the excerpt, concentrating on maintaining the tempo when the music suddenly becomes soft.

Problems In Vocal Production

Piano can be created by simply using a slightly slower flow of air but the air pressure must remain steady.

■ **Strategy for singers:** *Transfer the effective use of air flow in* forte *singing to* piano *singing.*

■ **Activity for singers:**
   a) Sing a phrase at a *forte* level. Notice the speed of the air flow.
   b) Repeat at a *piano* level, using a slower speed of air. If there is difficulty with the concept of air speed, think of the air moving more gently for soft music.
   c) Repeat, adjusting the air pressure as required to keep the pitch in tune.

Many singers feel that they need to hide some of the sound to become softer. In an effort to hide the sound, they may inadvertently change the tone quality and flatten the pitch.

Flat singing in *piano* passages can sometimes be cured by simply eliminating the negative things that can occur when singers "hide" the sound:
- Partially closed mouth;
- Voice placement too far back in the head;
- Poor vocal energy;
- Unfocused tone.

Suggestions to remedy each of these negative habits follow.

Open Mouth

Many singers automatically use a smaller mouth opening for *piano*. This does soften the sound but it also flattens the pitch.

- ■ **Strategy for singers:** *Do not use a smaller mouth opening for soft passages.*
- ■ **Activity for singers:** This activity gradually lets the singers become accustomed to keeping the mouth open for *piano* passages.
    - a) Alternate phrases at *forte* and *piano* levels, keeping the mouth open for both dynamic levels.

Si - lent night, ho - ly night; All is calm, all is bright round yon vir - gin

- b) Take a moment to relax the mouth.
- c) Repeat the same phrases with the mouth open, noticing that the physical sensation of vibrations is much more subtle when the music is at a *piano* level.
- d) Relax the mouth.
- e) Repeat the same phrases with the mouth open, matching the tone quality of each *piano* phrase with each *forte* phrase.
- f) Sing the entire passage at a *piano* level with the mouth open.

Forward Placement

As soon as the dynamics change to *piano*, many singers suddenly switch the vocal placement to the back of the head in an unconscious effort to "hide" the sound. However, when the vocal placement is too far back in the head, the pitch tends to be flat.

There are many ways to encourage the placement to be forward in *piano* passages but awareness is the first step. Whenever the dynamics are *piano*, singers should remember to keep the placement forward.

- ■ **Strategy for singers:** *Project the tone forward in soft passages.*
- ■ **Activities for singers:**
    1. While singing softly, imagine that a small ball of sound is spinning a few inches in front of your face.

    2. a) Sing a phrase loudly.
       b) Quickly place the hands beside the ears with the palms facing forward. Immediately repeat the phrase softly while moving the hands slowly forward. When the hands are moving forward, the vocal placement tends to stay forward.

Vocal Energy

In soft music, the sound often loses vitality and goes flat. If an appropriate energy level can be maintained, it is easier to keep the pitch up.

- ■ **Strategy:** *Keep the energy flowing in soft passages.*

■ **Activity for singers:**
    In a slow, soft piece:
       a) Sing a rhythm to each longer note:

       b) Repeat, singing the rhythms as written while imagining the inner rhythms.

The Circle Concept For Focused Tone

Soft music is sometimes out of tune because it has lost the focus of the pitch; it sounds fuzzy instead of soft. If singers imagine they are completely filling a small circle with sound as they sing, the pitch tends to be more focused. When the pitch is focused, it is easier for singers to compare the pitch with other singers and then make any necessary adjustments.

■ **Strategy for singers:** *Keep the tone focused by thinking of a circle of sound.*
■ **Activity for singers:**
    a) Sing a phrase loudly, imagining a large circle.

excerpt from *The Swallow* by Nancy Telfer [Kjos 8735]

       b) Repeat softly, imagining a small circle.

       c) Repeat, imagining the sound moving forward from the mouth in a small tube. The forward motion adds some momentum to the sound to keep the pitch up.

The Nature Of Dynamics

Many singers use only two levels of dynamics and each of those levels has only one meaning for them: *piano* = muted   *forte* = a blast!

Singers not only must become adept at using a variety of dynamics, but should also realize that each level of dynamics can be expressed in distinctively different ways in various pieces of music or within one piece of music. *Piano* dynamics can be described as being delicate, mysterious, distant, intense, or musically expressive in any number of other ways. When a *piano* passage becomes boring, it tends to be flat. When the singers understand the reason why the music is soft, the music comes alive without becoming louder and the tuning tends to be much better.

■ **Strategy:** *When a phrase is marked* piano, *make sure that the singers understand how the dynamics can affect the mood of that phrase.*

■ **Activity:**

Have the singers:

   a) Notice the change of dynamics:

excerpt from *Agnus Dei* by W.A. Mozart [Kjos 8736]

mi - se - re - re,   mi - se - re   -   re   no - bis.

   b) Determine the reason for the change in dynamics: playful variety? same lyrics but a different meaning expressed (e.g. loud wailing followed by a more personal plea)? a request from a heavy heart followed by a quiet, more spiritual approach? etc.
   c) Sing the music with reverse dynamics: first phrase *piano*; second phrase *mezzo forte.*
   d) Repeat with the dynamics as written in the music.

■ **Strategy for singers:** *Concentrate on one particular image to capture the mood of a* piano *passage.*

■ **Activity for singers:**

   a) Think of an image (e.g. a delicate flower) while singing soft music.
   b) Repeat with a different image (e.g. a jewel).
   c) Compare the intonation with the two images.

Other possible images: lace, a gentle breeze, moonlight.

■ **Strategy:** *To avoid mechanical use of dynamics:*
- Do *not* think of them separately from the intent of the music: e.g. "Sing softly here; *crescendo* at measure 67; *forte* at measure 69."
- Connect the dynamics with other musical elements (e.g. timbre, weight, intensity, meaning of the lyrics, etc.).

■ **Activity for singers:**
  a) Follow the dynamics as written in the music

excerpt from *Agnus Dei* by W.A. Mozart [8736]

  b) Try different ways to make the soft part more musical:
     i) Sing more lightly;
     ii) Sing with more intensity;
     iii) Make the lyrics sound more personal.
  c) Then choose the way that is most appropriate for this particular section of the music.

■ **Strategy:** *Link the music with an appropriate color.*
■ **Activity for singers:**
  a) Imagine a color while singing a section of a piece.
  b) Repeat with a different color.
  c) Compare the intonation of the two versions.

XIII. Singing Loud Music

With loud music, the pitch can easily become distorted. Some singers push the sound out, losing control and creating inconsistencies in the tuning. They may feel that the sound cannot be loud unless they force the maximum amount of effort from their mouths. The struggle to achieve a *forte* can be counterproductive because the tension created with the struggle actually reduces the level of sound.

The whole concept of what *forte* means needs to be examined. Depending on the particular effect needed, *forte* could be conceived as full, large, powerful, weighty, intense, or musically expressive in any number of other ways, but it should not be linked with tension or a blasting effect.

■ **Strategy for singers:** *Imagine a large circle for* forte. *Fill the circle with:*

excitement	a huge sound	solid power
sorrow	intensity	warmth

■ **Activity:**
While one singer stands some distance in front of the choir, have the choir:
a) Sing a *forte* passage.
b) Repeat, concentrating on filling up a large circle with an exciting sound.
c) Listen to comments from the listener.
d) Repeat, making any suggested changes.

When the vocal placement is in the back of the head, the voice sounds loud to the singer but softer and flatter to the audience. The singer must learn to release the sound forward and trust the physical sensation of the air pressure and the vibrations to know that the voice is sounding loud to the audience.

■ **Strategy for singers:** *Combine the circle concept and proper forward placement to keep the pitch centered.*
■ **Activity for singers:**
a) Sing a *forte* passage.
b) Repeat, concentrating on filling up a large circle with as much warmth as possible.
c) Repeat, concentrating on projecting the sound forward.
d) Repeat, using the large circle concept and good projection.
e) Repeat, memorizing the physical sensation.

XIV. Dynamics That Change Gradually

When the dynamics change gradually, it is sometimes difficult to keep the tuning consistent. In a *diminuendo* passage, the pitch may start to sink. In a *crescendo* passage, the pitch may start to become sharp. When the singers are aware of this intrinsic problem, they can be prepared to use preventative strategies.

- ■ **Strategy for singers:** *For a* diminuendo, *use a mind image to give an upward lift to the pitch.*
- ■ **Activity for singers:**
  During a *diminuendo*, keep the music spinning forward from the mouth toward a distant place. The spinning motion can add enough energy to keep the pitch up.

If necessary, point the spinning motion slightly upward rather than straight ahead. The pitch tends to keep up if the singer thinks "up."

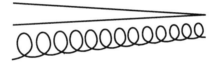

- ■ **Strategy for singers:** *For a* crescendo, *use a mind image for a stabilizing effect on the pitch.*

- ■ **Activity for singers:**
  During a *crescendo*, think of the sound expanding upwards and downwards at the same time.

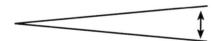

NOTE: a) If the conductor uses the term "rising dynamics," the pitch may start to rise, too. It is better if the singers think of expanding the dynamics rather than raising the dynamics. b) The conductor needs to establish the nature of the *crescendos* which will be used in each piece. A *crescendo* can be filled with excitement, suspense or agony; it can create a sweeping sensation or be expressive of any number of other musical ideas. Similarly, a *diminuendo* can be sad, exquisitely beautiful, calming, etc.

■ **Strategy:** *Explore the nature of a* crescendo *or* diminuendo *in a particular piece.*
■ **Activities:**

1. Use descriptive words to summarize the nature of a *crescendo*:
"gradually filling up the heart with sound"

excerpt from Cast Your Burden Upon the Lord by Felix Mendelssohn [Kjos 8738]

"becoming more and more intense"

excerpt from Cast Your Burden Upon the Lord by Felix Mendelssohn [Kjos 8738]

"like a beautiful flower unfolding"

excerpt from The Voice of My Weeping by Nancy Telfer [Kjos 8765]

2. Often one group of singers instinctively understands the nature of a particular piece of music. Have those singers demonstrate the nature of a *crescendo* in that piece.

3. Have the singers watch carefully as the conductor expresses a *diminuendo* by several different ways of conducting:
   a) Gradually relaxing the tension (arm becoming more relaxed and beat becoming rounder)
   b) Sound fading into the distance (hand very slowly moving forward)
   c) Sound gradually becoming warmer (left hand slowly coming closer to the right hand)

excerpt from Bogoroditse Devo by Sergei Rachmaninoff [Kjos 8840]

Make sure that the singers understand which interpretation will be used in concert. If the singers are not united on the interpretation of a *crescendo*, there can be difficulty with the tuning. Because each singer can view a *crescendo* in a different way, the individual tunings can be different (i.e. at the beginning of a bar some singers may be sharp while others are in tune; at the end of that bar, different singers may be sharp). When all these tunings are joined together, there may be some very interesting intonation problems as the sound becomes louder. If all the singers are using the same concept for the *crescendo*, it is much easier to address specific problems and keep the tuning uniform.

XV. Music With Sustained Notes

When music contains sustained pitches, the tuning of the sustained notes should be stabilized before work is done on fine-tuning the other pitches. The sustained notes can act as a stable framework; the other singers can then tune their moving parts with the sustained pitches.

■ **Strategy:** *To keep the singers concentrating on long, sustained pitches, encourage them to sing the pitch with more musical expression.*

■ **Activities:**

1. On a sustained note, have the singers keep the energy flowing forward to keep the pitch from becoming flat:

2. Have the singers feel the phrasing of the music as a whole while they sing a sustained pitch. This keeps the ear turned toward the tuning of the other parts.

excerpt from *There Shall A Star* by Felix Mendelssohn [Kjos 8773]

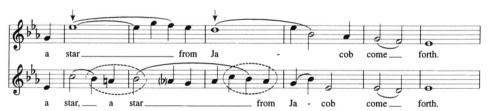

■ **Strategy:** *During a sustained pitch, concentrate on the physical sensation of the pitch.*

■ **Activity:**

Feel the physical place where the tuning seems to focus in the head and then concentrate on keeping that sensation.

■ **Strategy for singers:** *Use a mind image to keep a sustained pitch in place.*

■ **Activity for singers:**

a) Aim the tuning at an appropriate point in the hall (e.g. the conductor, the front row, a high spot on the back wall, etc.).

b) Lower the target (e.g. the conductor's waist instead of face, etc.) and notice how much more difficult it is to keep the pitch from becoming flat.

c) Raise the target, keeping the concentration steady for the duration of the pitch.

■ **Strategy:** *Use the sustained pitches in other parts to keep the tuning stable.*

■ **Activities for singers:**

1. As the choir sings a short section of the music, listen for sustained notes in other parts and tune with them.

excerpt from *There Shall A Star* by Felix Mendelssohn [Kjos 8773]

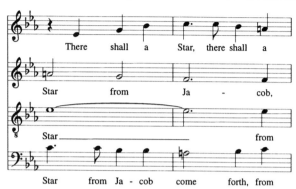

2. a) Bracket the sustained or repeated notes in other choral parts.
   b) Compare the tuning with the bracketed parts.

excerpt from *Can't You Hear Those Freedom Bells Ringing?* arr. by Lena McLin [Kjos 8763]

XVI. High Pitches

Effective Warmups

Everything is easier to tune when the voice is warmed up properly. Problems in tuning are most obvious in the lower and upper parts of the range when the voice is not yet warmed up. In the higher part of the range, the tuning changes with any slight adjustment of the vocal mechanism. Because of this, the singer must find exactly the right vocal placement for each pitch. The high pitches seem very close together. The pitches may be found with more precision when the voice is warmed up.

It is best to begin a warmup with pitches in the middle part of the range. After the midrange is warmed up, singers can proceed to go quickly and lightly to higher pitches and then descend to the middle again.

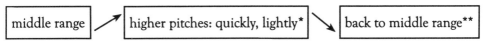

* Do not stay high too long at a time. Long high notes are difficult to sustain. It is less stressful to move about quickly on the higher pitches. When the voice is warmed up, it will be ready to work more seriously on high pitches with longer durations.

** After working on high pitches, it is important to give the singers an opportunity to sing some middle pitches so that the opening inside the mouth can return to a normal, less stressful position.

Keeping the Throat Relaxed

Poor tuning on high pitches is often the result of tension. When the throat is relaxed, it is easier to keep the pitch in tune. When a singer works hard, there is a tendency to become tense and the tuning becomes distorted. Singing should not seem like work. Short sessions on high-pitched music are best.

- ■ **Strategy:** *When intensive rehearsal is needed on high passages, isolate the aspect of the music that actually needs the work (e.g. rhythms, phrasing, pitches, dynamics, etc.).*
- ■ **Activities for singers:**
  1. Have the singers speak the rhythms.

excerpt from *Hallelujah Chorus* by G.F. Handel

  2. Have the singers sing the music an octave lower to learn the melodic contour and pitches.

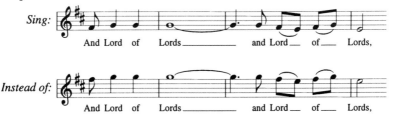

3. With a different high-pitched phrase, have the piano demonstrate the melodic phrasing while the singers sing along silently in their minds.

4. Have the singers speak the words in rhythm with the dynamics.

excerpt from *Bogoroditse Devo* by Sergei Rachmaninoff [Kjos 8840]

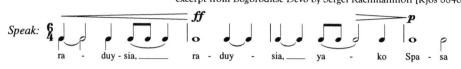

■ **Strategy for singers:** *Be relaxed before reaching the high pitches of a phrase.*
■ **Activity for singers:**
   a) Sing a broken chord pattern:

   b) Repeat, concentrating on relaxing the throat for the middle pitches and continuing, still relaxed, for the highest pitch.
   c) Repeat without raising the head for higher pitches. (The throat becomes tense when the head rises.)

NOTE: Do not continue for very long with the attention on the throat because the singers may become tense.

During adverse conditions (e.g. high pitches) singers can be trained to use relaxation techniques like the ones on pages 37-42 so that the pitch does not go sharp. Clenching a fist during a bar's rest before a high-pitched passage may be helpful for some singers (as long as they remember to relax the fist before they begin singing!). As the singers have one measure of rests, they can clench a fist for two beats and then relax for the two beats right before their entry. Some singers may prefer a relaxing visual image in their minds before singing high pitches.

Building Stamina

Poor tuning may also be the result of poor stamina. The singers may not be able to sustain control over the tuning of high pitches for very long. Even with singers who are in good general vocal shape, it is better not to sing high pitches for too long at one time because the tuning tends to become worse if the singers keep working at it for too long.

■ **Strategy:** *Increase the stamina for high pitches over several weeks.*
■ **Activities:**
   1. A few weeks before beginning stressful, high-pitched repertoire, start working on warmups which will build the stamina for high pitches.

2. Over a period of weeks, gradually lengthen the rehearsal time for high-pitched passages.

Balancing High Pitches With Low Pitches

It is easier to sing a high-pitched phrase in tune when it is sung with other choral parts or an accompaniment because:

- The low pitches in the other parts or accompaniment act as reference points for the high pitches.
- The singers can balance the tuning if the high pitches move in contrary motion with a bass line.
- The overtones of the lower pitches provide sympathetic support for the higher pitches. Singers are much more confident tuning high pitches when they feel the acoustical support of the lower pitches.

Unless it is necessary, singers should not sing high pitches without some supportive sounds from other voicings or the piano below them. However, it is often useful to remove inner parts to let the outer parts be heard more easily (e.g. soprano and bass alone or soprano and piano alone).

■ **Strategy:** *Listen intently to the lower pitches in other choral parts or the accompaniment.*

■ **Activities:**

1. Have the accompanist play while the singers imagine they are singing a high phrase.

excerpt from *Hallelujah Chorus* by G.F. Handel

Repeat with the singers singing the high phrase aloud, continuing to listen to the accompaniment.

2. Have the singers sing a high phrase with one lower choral part (or the piano accompaniment), balancing the tuning with the lower part.

excerpt from *Missa Brevis for Mixed Choir* by Nancy Telfer [Kjos 8760]

When the tuning has stabilized, add the other parts.

The Conductor's Gestures

For high pitches, some conductors raise the left hand in an upward gesture. If the conductor keeps the left hand in an elevated position during high passages, the singers may become tense. It is easier for the singers to keep the jaw relaxed and down with the throat open if the conductor uses a gesture positioned at a lower level. When the conductor's left hand is positioned at the level of the diaphragm, the singers often find it easier to provide more diaphragmatic support for high pitches.

XVII. Low Pitches

It is better to start work on intonation after the warmup is well under way because the voice is then more flexible and focused and the ears are beginning to hear the details of the sound better. After the middle part of the range is warmed up, the singers should begin some work with lower pitches. It is best to begin with a middle pitch and then move slowly down by step:

Because lower pitches speak more slowly than higher pitches, it is important to move more slowly in the lower part of the range during the warmup.

Low pitches, whether produced by a voice or an instrument, are generally more difficult to hear than high pitches. Singers tend to have the vocal placement too far back, making the lower pitches even more difficult to hear. Middle pitches often automatically use a more forward vocal placement which can be transferred to the lower pitches as the voice descends. When the voice placement is forward, the pitch is easier to hear and easier to tune.

When the vocal placement is too far back, the pitch often sounds flat. If the singers shift the placement forward and use a smaller focus, the pitch rises. A brighter timbre can also help make the pitch sound higher.

■ **Strategy for singers:** *Keep the vocal placement forward on lower pitches.*
■ **Activity for singers:**
    a) Sing a low-pitched phrase with "ee" or "ay":

    b) Repeat with the lyrics, keeping the placement forward and focusing the
    pitch at the front of the mouth.

excerpt from I'll Give My Love An Apple, Canadian folk song

■ **Strategy for singers:** *Keep the head in position to prevent the lower pitches from sagging.*

■ **Activity for singers:**

a) Sing a descending scale and let the head move downward with the lower pitches. Notice the flatness of the lower pitches.

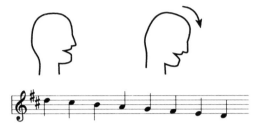

b) Repeat, keeping the head steady. Notice the improvement in the tuning.

■ **Strategy:** *Have the choir automatically brighten the timbre a bit on lower pitches.*

■ **Activity for singers:**

Memorize the bright timbre at the top of a scale and retain the brightness while descending through the lower pitches.

■ **Strategy:** *Balance the tuning of the low pitches with the higher pitches in another choral part or the accompaniment.*

■ **Activity:**

If a low-pitched line is out of tune, have that choral part practice the line with the soprano part rather than leaving the lower voices exposed with no higher part to act as a balance.

XVIII. Ascending and Descending Passages

Ascending passages tend to go sharp and descending passages tend to go flat. The music pushes the tuning in the direction of the pitches:

Generally, there tends to be a balanced number of ascending and descending passages. This helps keep the tuning from straying too far in one direction.

excerpt from *Can't You Hear Those Freedom Bells Ringing?* arr. by Lena McLin [Kjos 8763]

A rising phrase for the sopranos is often balanced by a simultaneous descending phrase in the bass part. The singers find it easier to balance the tuning with each other when this occurs.

excerpt from *Cast Your Burden Upon the Lord* by Felix Mendelssohn [Kjos 8738]

However, some music has predominantly ascending phrases. The composer may use this technique to create an uplifting or expectant effect for the listeners. This is an effective compositional technique but the choir must be very careful not to go sharp. Other music has descending phrases to express sorrow or comfort. In this music the choir can easily go flat. Most singers can learn to adjust to these inherent problems. When they are aware of intonation problems with ascending or descending passsages, they can be prepared to adjust the pitch when they see such music. However, choirs which are chronically sharp probably should avoid music with too many ascending passages. Choirs which are chronically flat probably should avoid music with too many descending passages.

■ **Strategy for singers:** *Consciously counteract the natural tendency to become flat.*
■ **Activity for singers:**
   Practice descending scales while thinking "up" as the pitch goes down.

■ **Strategy for singers:** *Consciously counteract the natural tendency to become sharp.*
■ **Activity for singers:**
   Practice ascending scales thinking "down" or "steady" as the pitch goes up.

XIX. Rhythmic Music

Using a Rhythmic Framework

Rhythms contain stressed and unstressed notes. The stressed notes provide a framework. If they are in tune, it is easier to tune the other pitches.

■ **Strategy:** *With groups of sixteenth notes, secure the rhythmic framework (the first pitch of each group of four notes) and then fill in the details (the inner rhythms).*

■ **Activity for singers:**

    a) Sing only the framework pitches.

    b) Sing every pitch but concentrate on the tuning of the framework.

    c) Repeat, listening more carefully to the inner pitches. The tuning problems may vary according to the repertoire (e.g. because a pickup pitch has the sensation of being "picked up," it is often tuned a bit too high). When the problem pitches are identified, they can be adjusted.

Enunciating the Words

In an effort to enunciate clearly in fast, rhythmic music, some singers overwork their mouth, lip, and tongue muscles. The music is easier to tune if the singers do not contort their mouths as they shape the consonants. Small, quick movements at the front of the mouth keep the basic shape of the cavity inside the mouth in a more consistent position for the vowels. With large movements of the mouth, it is easy to overreact to a pitch change and start too high or too low. With small, quick movements, the focus is smaller and the pitch has more clarity.

■ **Strategy:** *Use small, quick movements for consonants in fast, rhythmic music.*

■ **Activities for singers:**

    1. a) Place hands on the cheeks, with fingers pointing up.

       b) Sing a short, rhythmic section of rehearsal music, keeping lip and tongue movement to a minimum.

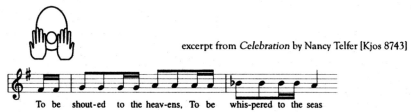

excerpt from *Celebration* by Nancy Telfer [Kjos 8743]

To be shout-ed to the heav-ens, To be whis-pered to the seas

    2. a) Place one hand about six inches in front of the mouth.

       b) Project the rhythms toward the hand, using minimum lip and tongue movement.

XX. Tempo

Music with a slow tempo goes flat more easily because there is not as much momen-tum to keep the pitch up. Music with a quick tempo can become sharp with the excitement of the speed. A wise tempo can help keep the music in tune.

■ **Strategy:** *If a slow piece tends to be flat, try increasing the tempo slightly. If the tone remains relaxed, the tempo will still sound slow.*

■ **Activity:**

Rehearse a slow piece at various tempos over a period of weeks. For the concert, the tendency to become flat may be counteracted by the excitement of the singers which may raise the pitch slightly. A moderate tempo may be the best choice in concert.

The reverse strategy may be employed for quick music which tends to be sharp: try using a slightly slower tempo. If the momentum and excitement are still present at the slower tempo, the music will still sound fast.

XXI. The Piano As a Tuning Aid

During early rehearsals, the piano should be situated to help the choir as much as possible. As the singers become less dependent upon the piano, it may be moved to a location suitable for the concert. Some useful tips follow.

Rehearsals

- It is better if the piano is not too far from the singers who have the most difficulty tuning.
- If the entire choir has intonation difficulties, the piano may be centered in front of the choir.
- The lid of the piano may be raised so that the sound carries better.
- Some conductors position a grand piano so that the sound is projected into the choir during a rehearsal.
- The accompanist may play a bit more loudly until the tuning is stabilized.

Concerts

- The piano should provide enough sound for the choir to tune properly.
- There should be a good balance between the choir and piano from the perspective of the audience.

Sometimes a compromise may be necessary with these two goals. If a sacrifice must be made, it is good to remember that most audiences prefer good intonation to good balance.

Tuning To Octaves

If the pianist is playing a single choral part, it is easier for the singers to tune if the pianist plays the part in octaves. When the piano is in unison with the singers, it is harder to hear the exact tuning of each pitch. With octaves, the singers can balance their part with the octave above or below. Soprano and tenor parts may be played on the piano with the octave below added to the pitches as written. Bass and alto parts should be doubled at the octave above.

■ **Strategy:** *When the accompanist is playing a single choral part, make the piano more audible by reinforcing the part at the octave.*

■ **Activity:**
  With any phrases that are difficult to tune, have the accompanist automatically play the part in octaves as the singers sing.

excerpt from *The Swallow* by Nancy Telfer [Kjos 8735]

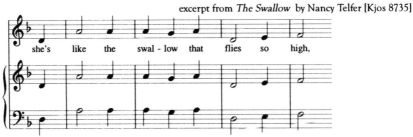

Occasional Help From the Piano

If the choir as a whole is sinking or rising in pitch, the pianist can help by providing a chord from time to time to bring the tuning to the attention of the singers.

■ **Strategy:** *Use the piano only at important moments to focus the ears of the choir on the tuning and to add energy to the pitch.*

■ **Activities:**

1. As the singers rehearse their repertoire, have the pianist play the chord on the first beat of each bar. The singers should make any adjustments as they hear the chord.

excerpt from *Gloria Sei Dir* by J.S. Bach [Kjos 8746]

2. During rehearsal, have the pianist play the chord whenever the harmony changes. If there is one particular place that continues to be a problem, the singers can circle the measure as a reminder.

excerpt from *Zigeunerlieder* by Johannes Brahms [Kjos 8780]

Listening During Breaths and Interludes

For a piano to be most effective, the choir must think of the piano as an integral part of the ensemble. When the choir is singing continuously, the singers should be listening for the accompaniment, adjusting the tuning to fit with the piano.

■ **Strategy:** *Have the singers tune with the piano whenever it is most audible.*

■ **Activities for singers:**

1. When breathing between phrases, listen for the piano and make any necessary adjustments in the tuning:

excerpt from "Celebration" by Nancy Telfer [Kjos 8743]

2. As each piano interlude ends, be careful to begin singing in tune with the piano. This may seem self-evident, but singers commonly begin to sing on a pitch that is slightly higher or lower than the pitch of the piano part because their concentration is directed toward vocal production, pronunciation or interpretation.

excerpt from *Celebration* by Nancy Telfer [Kjos 8743]

3. When it is difficult to hear the piano through the texture of the choral singing, mark the score where the piano <u>can</u> be heard, and use these markings as landmarks for checking intonation.

Tuning With an Organ

Many singers have difficulty tuning with an organ because they have not learned how to listen to the rich timbre created by multiple colors. Some registrations may sound like a wall of sound to them. When a choir is learning a piece, the organist may wish to:

• Rehearse with piano accompaniment until the tuning is stabilized;
• Use organ registrations that are easy to hear clearly; this varies from one organ to the next. When the piece is more stable, registrations appropriate for that particular piece may be used.

XXII. Tips For Conductors

The responsibility for good intonation is shared between the conductor and the singers. The conductor teaches the singers skills for good intonation and the singers are responsible for learning and using them effectively. The conductor is also responsible for a good physical and psychological environment to make good intonation easier to accomplish.

Choral Seating Plans
During rehearsals, a conductor may wish to use a formation and seating plan specially designed to help intonation.

Curved Formation
Sound travels in straight lines. When the sound is projected from a singer's mouth, it tends to travel forward in a funnel shape. As one singer sings, the singers on either side can hear the edges of the funnel. When the choir is seated in a curved formation:
- The funnels overlap more;
- Singers farther apart can hear each other's voices better. This, of course, helps more singers to tune more easily with each other.

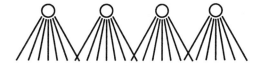 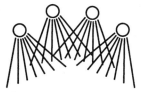

Sometimes there is not enough room to place the singers shoulder to shoulder and each singer must turn slightly toward the center. The head of each singer should be facing the same direction as the body, even though it may not be facing the conductor. If the face is turned sideways, the neck will be tense. A singer's face should be in line with the body but the eyes may turn toward the conductor.

Determining the Number Of Rows
Singers can hear the sound coming from the singers behind them much better than the sound from the singers in front of them. Two rows are easier to tune than one because each singer in the front row can hear the singers beside him or her and also several singers behind. Three rows work well, too.

However, if a choir has too many rows, then the tuning problems become more complicated. The sound can become muddy and the focus of the tuning may be lost. It is better to have several long rows than many short rows. In a classroom situation, this means that the students should be seated like this:

not this:

Risers

If the singers are all at the same level on the stage, it is more difficult for the choir to tune. When singers with good intonation are receiving all-encompassing sound in the back of the head, it is difficult for them to maintain the integrity of accurate tuning. If poor tuners are blasted with sound at the backs of their heads, they feel as if they are being "pushed about" by the sound. The singers feel as if there is a struggle with the tuning.

If the singers are placed on different levels on risers, the sound comes over the top of the head and it is acoustically and psychologically easier to fit the tuning into place.

Individual Placement Of Singers

During rehearsals, singers with poor intonation can benefit by sitting in front of good tuners or beside them. With this positioning, the model tuners can be heard more easily and the poor tuners can check their own progress on a regular basis. However, this works much better if the model tuner has a focused voice. Large voices, however well tuned, are not good models because the focus is too loosely defined to be easily matched.

Singers with excessive vibrato can disturb the general intonation of a choir. This problem can be alleviated by surrounding the disturbing voice with singers who naturally soak in the sound around them. This takes the edge off the vibrato and blends the pitches together better. e.g. If a soprano has excessive vibrato, the vibrato can be dampened by the close presence of other singers with large, mellow voices. It is often effective to place this soprano beside or in front of basses since it is fairly common to have basses who absorb the sound around them. If possible, place a soprano with a large, mellow voice in front.

Sectional Placement of Singers

For general tuning purposes, there are several reasons why the following seating arrangement is often used with SATB choirs:

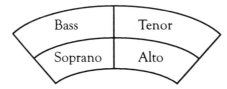

1. Because of the nature of the vocal types, many sopranos and tenors have a tendency to go sharp and many altos and basses have a tendency to go flat. If sopranos and tenors are placed together, they tend to "encourage" each other to go sharp. Altos and basses "encourage" each other to go flat.

When sopranos and basses are placed together, they tend to balance their natural tuning tendencies and can stay in tune more easily. The same is true for altos and tenors.

2. Sopranos and basses form the harmonic framework in music that is harmonically based. If these singers are close together, it is easier for them to solidify the tuning.

3. It is good to place the altos and tenors to the conductor's right. Because most singers hear intonation better in their right ears, the altos and tenors can hear the sopranos and basses better in this formation to fit in with the framework while the sopranos and basses tune to each other.

These general principles may be used with staggered choir formation, too, by generally keeping basses and sopranos together to the left of each grouping and alto and tenors together to the right.

```
BT  BT  BT  BT  BT
SA  SA  SA  SA  SA
```

Other formations may be useful for specific purposes. For example, if only one section in a choir has tuning problems, it needs to be placed in a situation where those singers can hear the other parts or the piano easily.

As a concert date approaches and the intonation is better, the seating plan may be adjusted to help the overall tone quality of the choir, the musicality of the ensemble, etc. Tuning is only one of several considerations for the concert placement.

The Conductor's Posture
The physical appearance of the conductor can affect the choir's tuning rather dramatically.

Conductor's Postural Problem	Affect On Singers
Weight not balanced evenly on both feet	Tuning becomes uncertain and more difficult to stay in the same key; sustained pitches tend to fluctuate.
Shoulders tense or high	Tendency to sing sharp
Conducting beat too high	Tendency to sing sharp
Imprecise beat	Pitch tends to fluctuate
Tense hands	Tendency to sing sharp
Slouched body	Tendency to sing flat
Unpleasant facial expression	Each singer reacts in a different way (sharp or flat); overall tuning tends to be poor.
Raised eyebrows	Tendency to raise the pitch; sometimes effective to correct flat singing.

Humidity
A humid day can cause singers with good intonation to sing out of tune. If nothing can be done about the humidity in the rehearsal space or concert hall, then singers must make the best of the situation: concentrate on the intonation and use strategies that are appropriate to the music.

Problems In Concert

Some choirs have good tuning most of the time in rehearsals but have difficulty during concerts. They need more experience with the challenges created during a concert. If the choir performs frequently, they should be aware of the tendency to go sharp (or flat) and be prepared to use the strategies they have learned to combat the problem. If the choir does not perform frequently, it can be very helpful during rehearsals to simulate some of the acoustical aspects of a concert situation.

■ **Strategy:** *Simulate a variety of possible concert acoustics during rehearsals so that the singers gain more experience in concert skills.*

■ **Activity:**

Practice with different acoustics by:

- Changing the positioning of the choir within the rehearsal room (e.g. face the side instead of the back of the room for some rehearsals or parts of rehearsals).
- Leaving a space between each singer.
- Changing the rehearsal venue occasionally (even if only by moving out into the hallway or stairwell to rehearse for fifteen minutes).

■ **Strategy:** *Have the singers practice being nervous in rehearsal, to gain experience in coping with the problem before the concert.*

■ **Activity:**

Because of nervousness, some choirs tend to be sharp in concert.

a) Make the singers nervous by talking intensely about performance anxiety, the importance of the concert, sweating, dry mouth, etc. before a sing-through.

b) Then have the singers apply what they have learned about correcting sharp singing during the sing-through.

c) During the sing-through, the conductor may wish to add further stress to the situation by standing too close to the singers, making weird noises, etc.

■ **Strategy:** *During a concert, make technical adjustments in the tempo or dynamics to make the tuning easier.*

■ **Activities:**

1. When rehearsal experience indicates that the singers may be flat, use a faster tempo in concert. For sharp singing, use a slower tempo.

2. To correct sharp singing in concert, use softer dynamics, and to correct flat singing, sing more loudly.